What Are We Doing?

"It began to get serious when
I was stopped dead in the center lane
of the Santa Monica freeway.
Traffic was bumper-to-bumper
with no relief in sight.

I looked up at the 30-foot wide
marquis billboard placed by
Caltrans in the center divider.
Electric lights spelled out
the message,

'Maintain your speed.'

That's when it came to me.
Why was I sitting here in my car?
To drive to an office to use a computer!
Why? I had one just like it at home—
with a modem to boot!

Telecommuting was born
on the freeway."

*

JACK M. NILLES
Father of Telecommuting

Other Works by Lis Fleming:

Electronic Cottage Handbooks
Electronic Cottage Report
Planners' Guide to Telecommuting
*Managing the One-Minute Commuter**

Troubleshooting Grades K thru 6
— A Handbook for Parents and Teachers

**Forthcoming companion to The One-Minute Commuter*

The
One-Minute
Commuter

Lis Fleming

How to Keep your Job
and Stay at Home
Telecommuting

For Tova who's growing up with it.
For David who's making it happen.
Happy telecommuting.

Fleming, LTD
P.O. Box 1738
Davis, CA 95617-1738

ISBN: 1-877887-14-5

For orders contact:
Acacia Books
1309 Redwood Lane
Davis, CA 95616
(916) 753-1519

Contents

Contents continued—

Driver's Test for the One-Minute Commuter

Driver Training for Company Programs

Introduction

You can do a good job for your company and do right by your family, too.

Balancing family and work is tough. The millions of you who raise a family, work 40 hours a week and face 2-hour commutes 5 days a week have my unflagging admiration. I'm not sure I could do it. But I am sure, that many of you don't *have* to do it.

The hard-working couple in this book, like many of you, travel to jobs every day. They have come to the hard choice: sacrifice family or sacrifice career.

Many of you have no choice at all—every penny is needed. And so you agonize. You worry about latchkey kids at home on their own and about children who go to school sick because you have to be at work.

This is one way telecommuting can help. One-minute commuters keep their jobs and stay at home to work. It's good for employees and good for the company. This book will tell you why and how you can get there.

Whether you're the employer or the employee, you can have a job *and* a life—and do a good job at both.

Lis Fleming

"Commuting is the single most

anti-productive thing we do."

*

ALVIN TOFFLER

Getting

Off to

the Right

Start

"Commuting to office work

is obsolete. It is now infinitely

easier, cheaper and faster to . . .

move information . . . to where

the people are."

*

PETER F. DRUCKER

What to Expect.

Learning to drive and learning to be a one-minute commuter are much alike. Remember when you learned to drive? You didn't just jump into the car, turn on the ignition and speed down the road. (At least, not if you followed the rules!)

Driver's license. To get your license you had to read a driver handbook, take a written test for a learner's permit and practice driving with a licensed driver in the car. You even had your eyesight tested. Finally you had to take and pass a driving test before you were issued your passport to freedom— the driver's license.

One-minute commuter's license. There is another passport to freedom — your license to telecommute. No law requires it. But you'll be a much better driver (telecommuter) if you learn the rules and practice the one-minute commuting exercises in the Driver Handbook. And you'll know how to avoid accidents. No, you won't have a fatal crash, but there are pitfalls that can trip up the unwary.

Avoiding pitfalls. You won't want to be the person who in a spurt of excitement moved all his equipment out of the office and set up at home. He had to move everything right back again after a few weeks because he simply didn't know what he was doing.

You won't want to be one of the women who gave up employee status to work at home and found themselves in an electronic sweatshop situation. They had to quit and file suit against their employer.

This book wasn't written at that time, but reading it could have saved these people and many others like them a great deal of time and trouble.

Looks easier than it is. Driving a car looks so easy. And once you have the hang of it, it becomes second nature to you. The law does require you to renew your license by having your eyesight checked and taking the written test again to make sure you remember the rules.

Telecommuting looks easier than it is. Once you have the hang of it, you'll find it a normal part of your life and wonder what all the fuss was about this way to work. But just like driving your car, you'll need to review the rules from time to time. Do this quarterly to make sure you're on the right track.

Expert advice. The rules you'll learn in this book come from the experts. Who are the experts? Some are telecommuters who learned the hard way. Mostly they are consultants who have trained hundreds of people (telecommuters and their managers and supervisors) over the past few years. My own experience with managing work at home and with telecommuting is combined here with the experience of others. You'll have at your fingertips the best information from the most reliable sources available.

Twenty questions. To get you off to the right start, here are the twenty questions people ask most often about telecommuting — and some quick answers to those questions. Knowing what to expect will make you a better one-minute commuter.

Telecommute

Is it a car phone
or a phone car?

Questions Most Often Asked.

1— *Do I have to have a computer?* No. Even though we tend to think of computers when we talk about telecommuting, all you really need is a telephone so the people at work can get in touch with you. Some workers go home to read. Others only need paper and pencil. It all depends on what kind of work you take home.

2— *Do I have to stay home all the time?* No. Most telecommuters spend some time in the central office. Some go in once a week for staff meetings. Others split their time between the main office and home. Some work at home only during certain projects. Because the place where you work is flexible, telecommuting is also called "flexiplace."

3— *Can I change back if I don't like it at home?* Yes. By all means tell your supervisor telecommuting is not working out and you want to come back to the central office. When you read the Driver Handbook, you'll discover ways to prevent that situation from happening. You'll find out ahead of time if working at home is for you and how many days you need to be in the central office to avoid isolation and other possible problems. Be sure to give yourself a few weeks to adjust.

4 — *How can I convince my employer to allow it?* That's what this book is all about. Follow the six steps in the Driver Handbook, and you'll learn how to do this. The secret is to let management know how telecommuting helps the company.

5 — *Won't I get out of touch with the office?* Not if you do it right. By following the instructions in the Driver Handbook, you'll set up ways to keep in touch with your co-workers and with your supervisor. Managers report that telecommuters often stay in touch better than co-workers who are in the central office every day.

6 — *Won't I give up my chances for promotion?* No. So far research indicates that telecommuters and their work are noticed more than when they were in the office all the time. Many telecommuters have been promoted because of this. It's too early to tell what will happen over the long term. Things may even out when telecommuting is common place.

7 — *Do I give up benefits when I work at home?* No. Telecommuters have the same salaries and benefits as any other employee. It's really no different from working in a branch office instead of the main office.

8— *What if my home is too small for telecommuting?* Telecommuters don't always work at home. They can work anywhere that's convenient. That could mean the community library, a room in a local business building with extra space, or an office in your neighborhood shopping center. Some condominiums and apartments are being built with shared office space on the ground floor. Many experts believe that in the future we will be working mostly in neighborhood offices. Check around to see if there are any affordable alternatives where you live.

9— *What if I belong to a union?* It all depends. Some unions fear sweatshops and simply say *no* to any kind of home work. Other unions help write the rules for their members to telecommute. They think of it as flexiplace and treat it the same as any other flexible scheduling.

10— *What should I do about electronic sweatshops? These can happen anywhere. Watch for the following: Workers are under constant surveillance. Keystrokes are electronically monitored and phone calls are listened to and timed. Workers are under constant pressure to produce. Sometimes they are assigned independent contractor status without benefits. These practices can damage your health and your morale. Don't agree to work at home or anywhere else under these conditions.*

11— What if all my work can't be done at home? You can still be a telecommuter. Don't rule yourself out as a candidate for telecommuting without going through the steps in the Driver Handbook. Tasks can be divided up into those that can be done at home and those that have to be done in the office.

12— Is telecommuting happening? Yes, it's alive and growing. When the idea of telecommuting first hit the press, people were talking about empty skyscrapers and deserted central cities (which didn't happen). That's not the way it works. Telecommuting is quietly spreading across the nation, changing the way we work.

13— Does telecommuting really save time? Yes. If your daily commute is 30 minutes each way, you spend 6 40-hour work weeks going to and from work. If you telecommute 2 to 3 days a week, you can save yourself 3 working weeks of driving. If you telecommute all 5 days a week, you'll save 6 working weeks a year.

14— Who pays for equipment? It depends. Usually, the employer provides equipment for workers. However, many telecommuters have volunteered their own phones and home computers because they wanted to start telecommuting right away.

15 – *Can I save on child care if I telecommute?* Yes, but with a word of caution. Telecommuting allows you to work at home when your children are sick and to be there working when they come home from school. You can save on child care for young children because they won't need as many hours of care as when you commute long distances to work. Don't expect to work full time at home and take care of children at the same time. Both you and your work will suffer.

16 – *Can I take a tax deduction for my home office?* Probably not. Telecommuting is voluntary and therefore does not appear to be a condition required for you to work. You are not in business for yourself. Chances are those rules won't change. Check with your tax preparer or the IRS about such matters.

17 – *What if I work with classified information?* It all depends. Research shows that secret information is generally as safe as the person who handles it regardless of where that person is. Location is not so much a factor. Hackers have broken into computers in banks and even the Pentagon. Your employer may say *no.* Or your employer may allow you to take the work home provided you follow certain rules of caution. Sometimes you'll take non-classified work home and do the classified work in the central office.

18— *Will I need a second telephone line at home?* Sometimes. If you'll be receiving calls from clients or will be staying in constant touch with the office, you should get a second line. Most dwellings are already wired for two or three lines. If you are working at home to get away from interruptions, then you may not want a second line.

19 — *Do employees have to telecommute?* No, not for home office telecommuting. Working at home must be voluntary or it doesn't work for you or your company. For programs where you work at neighborhood offices rented by your company, the answer is most likely *yes*.

20— *What if my manager says no?* You can't telecommute unless your manager agrees, but keep trying. Check your Driver Handbook for the list of indicators that signal your company is receptive to telecommuting. You'll find several activities you can use in your campaign.

Meet the One-Minute Commuters.

Ann and Tom Jacobs.

Ann and Tom Jacobs live in the desert on the far edge of Los Angeles where the affordable homes are. They work hard to pay for that little white house. They are working to achieve the "American Dream," a house of their own. Here is their story—very much like that of millions of other Americans.

The situation. It seemed they were never home except to sleep. Ann commuted to her accounting job in two hours of bumper-to-bumper traffic after taking two-year-old David to day school. Tom drove the old blue VW to his marketing job, taking the freeway in the opposite direction. It took him 90 minutes on a good day.

They reached home at seven-thirty in the evening, sometimes later if they stopped for groceries. After they got David to bed and had dinner, the day was gone. They would set the alarm to beep at four-thirty before the sun rose.

Once in a while David would forget and call Mrs. Nelson, the daycare supervisor, "Mommy." They still felt bad about missing his first steps. Their second baby was due in four months, and they would have even more demands on their time. They already felt as if they didn't have time to be a family.

What they wanted. Tom and Ann desperately wanted more time for the family. They wanted to keep their house and to drive less to get to work. They needed two incomes to support the family. They liked their jobs and wanted to keep them rather than trying to find new jobs closer to home. Ann very much wanted to be home with the new baby. They wanted to spend more time with David and with each other.

Hard choices. Should Ann give up her job? That would mean giving up the house and moving to an apartment near Tom's work. Could they even find an apartment they could afford in a neighborhood that was right for children? What should they do?

Telecommuting discovered. Tom first discovered telecommuting by reading the Sunday paper. He told Ann about the article and how telecommuting was used for doing information work. They both read the article from beginning to end.

Ann and Tom spent an entire Sunday with a yellow note pad and pencils working out how telecommuting might work for them. It was Ann who came up with the idea of calling themselves one-minute commuters.

She told Tom, "What if we turned the extra bedroom into a home office? It would take only a minute to get to work instead of two hours. We could become one-minute commuters."

Saving time. They looked at the commuting time chart in the paper and figured out how much time they could save if their commute was one minute instead of two hours. With the extra time, they really could take David to the park, jog in the mornings, go out to dinner with friends, have family picnics, or even take a night class.

Child Care. There was a family daycare home in the neighborhood where David could stay while they worked. When David was ill one of them could work at home instead of being absent and using sick leave.

Ann thought she could work at home during the last month of pregnancy without overdoing it. She would gradually begin working again part-time when the new baby was a few weeks old. In that way they wouldn't have to be entirely without her paycheck for several months while she was on parental leave.

Saving Money. Tom wanted to know how much money they could save by being one-minute commuters. So they made a list: gas, oil, car repairs, extra insurance, parking, lunches out and extra business clothes. They were amazed at how much money they spent just going to work. If they could save on those things, Ann could afford to work part-time.

Working it out. Ann and Tom didn't have a Driver Handbook for one-minute commuters to follow. Like millions of others they had to work it out for themselves. Fortunately, they had come across a very useful article in the paper. They took their time and did a lot of careful planning.

Convincing management. Ann Jacobs was ready to give it a try. She took her proposal to her manager, Ms. Miller. They talked it over.

After thinking about it for awhile and talking with other managers in the company, Ms. Miller agreed that using Ann's maternity leave to test one-minute commuting would be an excellent idea.

In fact, the company had been worried about what they would do without Ann. She was a key employee and the only one who knew the accounting system well. They welcomed her continuing to work part-time. It would save a lot of disruption.

Ms. Miller also felt it would improve the chances that Ann would stay with the company after the birth of her second child. This was the time when most mothers would not return to work even though they had planned to do so. The company had invested in Ann and wanted to retain her.

So Ann set up her home office in the spare bedroom. With a company computer and modem, she began telecommuting four days a week until the baby was born. (It's a girl— Angela!)

After the first month, Ann began working three hours each day while the baby slept. In a few months when Angela becomes mobile, she will join her older brother David at the daycare home down the street four hours each afternoon.

Convincing management. Tom Jacobs approached his employer with a proposal to work at home. Mr. Howard, an entrepreneur at heart and owner of the marketing firm, thought one-minute commuting was an interesting idea.

Since Tom managed the work of several others in the graphic arts department, Mr. Howard said he could establish his own schedule so long as he would guarantee that work was done on time and with the usual high quality. It would be up to Tom to be available for staff meetings and to consult with clients. Mr. Howard expected Tom to keep him posted on his schedule and on projects.

So Tom began to look for telecommuting openings. Once when he had the flu, he worked on a project at home while he recovered. He wrote the results in a memo and sent it to Mr. Howard. Later, a rush project came in. He took it home over the weekend and stayed there on the following Monday to finish. Again, he wrote it up in a memo.

The company bought a fax machine for Tom to co-design art work by long-distance. Later Mr. Howard asked him to write a company policy on telecommuting because other employees began asking for permission to telecommute.

Eventually, Tom hopes to set up a formal program getting the company to rent office space for him in the neighborhood shopping center. In the meantime, he enjoys those days during the month when there is a project to take home. He works at his fold-away drawing table in a corner of the living room and has lunch on a workday with Ann and the children.

Cindy Walters.

The situation. Cindy Walters worked for a New York city accounting firm and made errors in her work every afternoon. There was a tight feeling in the pit of her stomach and it was impossible to work. The problem was that school was out. She wouldn't be able to concentrate on her work until four o'clock when she would call home to make sure Lisa and Jason were safely in the apartment.

Working it out with telecommuting. Cindy convinced her supervisor to let her leave the office every afternoon at two-thirty, taking her work home to finish. This was to be on a trial basis. She met her children at school, and they walked home together. While Jason and Lisa did their homework, Cindy worked on her home computer. She uploaded her work into the company mainframe in the evening after office hours. Her supervisor was pleased. Not only did Cindy do her work without errors, but she got much more work done than she had before telecommuting.

Comment. Workers like Cindy Walters have to get permission from their supervisors (and sometimes the permission of their supervisor's supervisor) to work at home. Cindy's supervisor could easily have said *no*. The Driver Handbook can help by giving you answers for supervisors.

We don't hear much about
latchkey kids these days.

They're not making headline news,
but they haven't gone away.

Millions of them
spend three or four hours a day
on their own.

Some lock themselves in at home.
Some wait in libraries.

Most hang out in malls
and on the streets.

Getting into what?

*

Telecommuting lets us be there
for our kids.

George Harris.

The situation. George Harris, manager of a Seattle financial firm, often spent Monday mornings peering at stalled traffic through a raindrenched windshield. This Monday, like too many Mondays before, the weekly staff meeting would begin without him, and the progress report he was to present would lie inside the briefcase on the passenger seat.

He consoled himself that his people at least knew he was stuck in traffic because of yet another accident on the bridge. He thought it was ironic that investing in a cellular phone allowed him to cancel appointments he couldn't get to on time.

Working it out with telecommuting. George decided to forget about going to the office on Mondays. Instead he arranged to do his planning and scheduling work at home. He took part in the staff meeting by speaker phone, faxing his report ahead for the secretary to copy and distribute.

Comment. Managers like George Harris can make decisions about one-minute commuting on their own. That doesn't mean they shouldn't read the Driver Handbook and complete the Driver's Test that follows it. Telecommuting can create problems for staff and co-workers if it's not carefully planned. Considering how others are affected is extremely important.

What

Where

When and

Why

"Californians waste

300,000 hours in traffic delays

every single workday."

*

KIRK WEST
President
California Chamber of Commerce

What Is Telecommuting?

Telecommuting is the end of the daily commute. It means working from home or from an office very near your home instead of commuting to a distant workplace. You use your telephone instead of your car to get to work. You trade your daily drive for your disk drive, if you use a computer.

The word telecommuting. The word was first coined by Jack M. Nilles in 1972. *Tele* refers to telecommunications technology and *commuting* refers to the daily trip a person takes to work.

Technology substitute. Telecommuting is a substitute for commuting in which work is moved to people instead of moving people to work. Technology such as the telephone, fax or modem is used to work at home or a neighborhood office instead of commuting to a central worksite by car, bus or train.

One-minute commuting. Since it only takes a minute to walk down the hall to your home office, you become a *one-minute commuter* on the days when you do your job at home. One-minute commuter is just another way to say telecommuter.

Who Is Telecommuting?

Telecommuters are ordinary people who work from home usually 1 to 4 days per week. They are salaried employees with regular benefits using the home (or a near-home satellite office) as a worksite.

Jobs at home. This is a growing trend. Just how many people work at home varies from study to study and according to how homebased work is defined. Estimates range from a low of 1 million to a high of 30 million. A 1989 survey by Link Resources, a New York research firm, found 26.4 million home workers. The survey also found that the number of people working at home grew exponentially during the past three years.

Entrepreneurs. Today about 15 million homebased workers are entrepreneurs with businesses of their own. These people are not usually counted as telecommuters.

One-Minute Commuters. Another 15 million home workers are employees who take their jobs home from 1 to 5 days a week. These are the pioneers of a flexible new work option called telecommuting. They have the paycheck and benefits of the employee and enjoy the flexibility and control of the entrepreneur.

Corporate telecommuting programs. A few of the many American companies using telecommuting include: AT&T, IBM, Pacific Bell, Computerland, Honeywell, Control Data, US West, Citibank, Digital Equipment, JC Penney, New York Life, American Express, Crum & Forster, Montgomery Ward, Bell-South, Equitable Life, Blue Cross/Blue Shield, Hewlett-Packard, Mountain Bell, and Travelers Insurance.

Government telecommuting programs. Telecommuting began as a private sector practice, but government is now taking a leadership role. The State of California; the City of Fort Collins, Colorado; the New York Port Authority; the City of Los Angeles; the Southern California Association of Governments; the County of Los Angeles; and the state of Washington all either have telecommuting programs or demonstration pilots.

Future of telecommuting. The number of telecommuters is expected to reach far beyond the 15 million originally predicted to be telecommuting by the year 2000. People facing the task of balancing work and family are learning how to become telecommuters. Governments are passing traffic ordinances requiring employers to reduce work trips. New technologies are making telecommuting easier.

The Information Age.

We are now in the information age. That means most of our work is no longer manufacturing products in the factory. In fact over 60 percent of our work has to do with information. Most of us are doing work that involves creating, processing and moving information in one way or another.

The electronic cottage. In the information age, people are beginning to work in the "electronic cottage" described in Alvin Toffler's classic *The Third Wave*.

"Electronic" refers to computers, telephones, answering machines, fax machines, copiers and other electronic equipment. The word "cottage" refers to the home — "cottage industry" is the term we have long used to describe homebased work or business.

The virtual office. The advent of electronic equipment makes it possible for much of today's work to be done anywhere. People have telephones in their automobiles, use fax machines in hotels and work on laptop computers in airplanes. With information age technology it's not necessary to travel to a central office to do work.

Why We Are Still Commuting.

We are still commuting because our management practices haven't caught up with the information age. We still run offices in the same way we ran factories.

The industrial age. It was necessary for workers to come to the factory to use the huge machinery that manufactured products. Smelting steel, assembling cars and refining oil are examples of industrial age jobs. Today just 3 percent of us do this kind of work.

The information age. Today most of us are doing office work, but we still commute to the central office just as if it were a factory. It's simply a habit. We follow a pattern that has been in place for the last 150 years.

The age of agriculture. Before the industrial era, 97 percent of us worked in agriculture. For centuries, we lived and worked on the farm. In those days most of us worked at home. Even those who had shops in town lived in a flat above the store.

Back to the future. Telecommuting takes us full circle, back to the work style of centuries ago. There is a big difference though. We are not isolated as were the farmers of old. Our technology keeps us instantly in touch with our employer and with the world.

What's Wrong with Commuting.

Information age technology makes it possible to move work to people rather than moving people to work. That makes much of our commuting unnecessary.

Commuting is wasteful. It wastes time, money and resources. Why spend two hours in bumper-to-bumper traffic to go somewhere else to use a telephone or computer or to hand someone a report that could be faxed in minutes? Why waste money and gasoline on trips we don't need to make? Why waste tax money on ever-more expensive freeways that fill up with cars as soon they are finished?

Commuting is unhealthy. Most of the pollutants in our air come from auto emissions. The more we drive, the worse the air we breathe, and the greater the danger to our health. Pollutants in the air also damage crops we eat and the water we drink. Driving on crowded highways is just plain dangerous.

Commuting is stressful. Fighting traffic takes a daily toll on us. We are tired when we get to work, and even more tired when we reach home at night. We are irritable, have trouble concentrating on our work and are less productive because of commuting stress. We have less time for interests that help us relax when we spend so much time driving long hours in heavy traffic.

Commuter Time Table.

How much time does your daily commute take? How much commuting do you really need to do? How much time could you save by telecommuting? How would you use your extra time? Consider the possibilities!

Daily one-way minutes	Daily round-trip minutes	Hours per year	Equivalent number 40-hour weeks
10	20	80	2
20	40	160	4
30	60	240	6
40	80	320	8
50	100	400	10
60	120	480	12

Figures are adjusted for vacation, holidays and sick leave time normally taken during a year. Source: Working from Home

Are you surprised? Others will be too. Show this chart around the office at break or lunch time. Most people don't realize how commuting time adds up. One-minute commuting can put more hours in your life.

Information Work.

Information work is simply doing something with information. Telling it to others over the phone, entering data, word processing, sending it by mail or fax, researching, analysing or planning—in short any way in which we handle information is information work.

Jobs done by one-minute commuters. This can be just about any kind of information work. Examples of the many jobs that can be telecommuted include: legal work, programming, graphic art, word processing, data entry, data processing, writing, claims processing, claims adjustment, medical advising, planning, sales, buying, management, supervision, economics, analysis, transcription (legal and medical), typesetting, research, civil service, politics, foreign language translation, auditing, any kind of brokering (information, stock and real estate), and much more.

Parts of jobs can be telecommuted. Most information tasks can be telecommuted. This means that many other jobs can be sorted into tasks that have to be done at the central location and information tasks that can be done at a home office. It isn't necessary for an entire job to be telecommutable in order to telecommute. You can do some tasks at the central office and take the rest home.

How Telecommuting Helps You.

You get more satisfaction. Most telecommuters feel that the highest benefit they gain is more control over their lives and their work. They feel trusted by their company and take more pride in their work. They have more time for their personal lives and can better balance family and work.

Telecommuting is loaded with benefits. Which of these benefits reported by one-minute commuters would help you if you were to work at home?

—*Reduced stress from the daily commute.* One-minute commuters report that they feel much better when they don't have to commute every day. In fact, some even say they look forward to the drive when it's their day in the central office.

—*Reduced commute time.* One-minute commuters save 2 to 4 hours a day depending on the length of their daily commute. This adds up to several work weeks during the year—a lot of extra time!

—*More time with family.* One-minute commuters get to see their kids in the school play during the workday and have time to just talk during dinner.

— *More time for outside activities.* One-minute commuters take a break to work out at the local gym, have time for the community theater group and volunteer at the neighborhood school.

— *More options for meeting child care needs.* One-minute commuters can work at home when their children are ill, and they avoid the worry of latchkey kids. Their children (even teenagers) check in with them after school.

— *Greater flexibility in scheduling.* One-minute commuters don't take a day off to wait for the plumber; they just do their work at home while they wait.

— *Fewer interruptions during work.* One-minute commuters can finish projects in half the time and with better quality because no one drops in to disrupt their concentration.

— *Working at your peak time.* Night owls can work late at night if they like. Telecommuters get more done in 4 hours of peak time than in 8 hours of the "blahs."

— *Savings on travel, food and clothing.* Telecommuters save on gas, parking, auto repair and transit fares by not driving to work every day. They save on restaurant lunches and buy fewer business suits since jeans and a sweatshirt are great at home.

What Telecommuters Say.

Here's what telecommuters have to say about why they became one-minute commuters and how their lives are better because of it. These statements are from real people in real jobs just like yours. After that we'll hear from real managers and supervisors, hopefully just like yours.

Legal transcriber.

"My daughter has a handicap and had to be in very expensive specialized daycare every workday. She is much happier spending some of those days at home with me while I work in my home office. Because my job requires me to produce a certain number of pages every two weeks, monitoring my work is easy for my supervisor. Working from home three days a week saves money and gives me more time for my daughter. I feel much better about my life and my work."

Event organizer.

"I used to bike to work. When I moved I had to drive an hour and a half. My work involves a lot of planning and writing which I can easily do on my home computer. Since my employer is concerned with health and clean air, my telecommuting allows us to set an example for the business community by reducing work-related employee trips."

Telecommunications manager.

"When my daughter is sick, I work at home on projects that need concentration such as plans for new telecommunications equipment and training workshops for implementing the new systems. Telephone messages are taken by the receptionist in exactly the same way as when I travel to conduct workshops."

Programmer.

"My supervisor and I both work from home because there is simply no office space for us at the university. I take home a terminal three days a week to do the programming. I bring it back, load the work into the mainframe and get my next assignment. I enjoy the quiet of my home office and avoid dangerous driving on foggy winter days."

Actuary.

"Severe allergies make it necessary for me to live in another city 500 miles away. It would have taken management months to find and train someone to replace me. I do sophisticated statistical analysis using a computer in my home office and fly to meetings at the central office twice a month. Because my skills are hard to find, my employer and co-workers are willing to schedule around me. It's working very well."

Manager.

"My wife is facing a long recovery from a severe illness. She dreaded staying day-after-day for months at a time in a nursing facility. She can stay at home so long as someone is there to help her. Until she is well enough to take care of herself, I work from my home office. I'm the manager of several architects, and we stay in touch by telephone and fax. I go in for periodic meetings, and work is going smoothly."

Word processor.

"I have young children who seldom saw me because I worked the late shift. My employer established a homebased telecommuting program because it was hard to get and keep people to work late. There was a lot of absenteeism, and we were always having to train new people. I set up a terminal at home and can now work at any convenient time of the day so long as I fill my quota on time. We have a certain amount of work to do each week and send it to the central office by modem. Things are much better both at work and at home."

How It Helps Your Company.

Telecommuting is loaded with benefits for the company. Because it often represents a change in the way supervisors manage, your employer won't want to let you telecommute unless you can show that there are sound business benefits for the company. Don't worry! There are lots of proven benefits other companies have realized from telecommuting.

— *Improved productivity by 15-30 percent.* Managers consistently report that the quantity and quality of work done by telecommuters goes up by an average of 20 percent.

— *Reduced cost of office space.* Home telecommuters provide their own office space. Rents for commercial offices are high and space made available adds up!

— *Improved morale.* Managers report employee morale consistently goes up along with performance. Telecommuters thrive on independence.

— *Improved management.* Managers of one-minute commuters must set clear goals and measure the results of work done. As they become better managers, productivity of both telecommuters and central office staff goes up. Telecommuters also become adept at managing their work and time.

— *Cutting commute trips.* Employers can comply with new laws that require reducing the number of work trips employees make. One-minute commuters reduce work trips and save money. Compare telecommuting savings to the cost of buying a commuter van and paying a driver.

— *Increasing staff without adding space.* Because one-minute commuters use less space at the central office, they make space available for new employees.

— *Off-peak use of computer equipment.* Because one-minute commuters often choose to work late nights or early mornings, they can access computer systems when no one else needs them. This avoids expensive delays.

— *Improved recruiting.* By offering telecommuting, companies find they can recruit people who otherwise would turn them down because of the long commute.

— *Reduced absenteeism.* One-minute commuters rarely miss a day's work. They work at home when children are ill. They even put in some hours when they don't feel well enough to make the drive to work. This is especially true for those who don't feel well in the morning and then have an "11 o'clock recovery," too late to drive to work.

—*Access to new labor pools.* By offering telecommuting, companies facing worker shortages can hire experienced people who are not otherwise available. Retired seniors, mothers with young children and the homebound disabled are productive at home.

—*Reduced relocation costs.* Valued employees who don't want to move when the company does, stay where they are and become telecommuters, saving the company thousands of dollars in relocation costs.

—*Less office socializing.* Employers find that a little time at the water cooler goes a long way. One-minute commuters don't chat away personnel dollars.

—*Fewer work interruptions.* Managers report that one-minute commuters get more work done with higher quality because work is not constantly interrupted.

—*Reduced turnover.* One-minute commuters are loyal to their companies. They seldom quit since their work schedules give them flexibility in meeting the needs of their personal lives.

—*Reduced cost of training replacements.* Because one-minute commuters seldom quit, the company saves thousands of dollars in recruiting and training replacements.

— *Reduced need for parking space.* Parking space is almost impossible to find in some cities. Parking also costs employers money even when employees pay monthly fees. High office space rental prices reflect the cost of expensive commercial property used for parking.

— *Incentive for overtime and shiftwork.* Companies typically have trouble hiring and retaining workers for late shifts. They have no problem getting and keeping one-minute commuters who don't have to leave home at night.

— *The bottom line is telecommuting saves money.* When planned and managed properly, telecommuting is inexpensive to establish, saves the company a good deal of money over the years, and improves both employee and management performance.

What Managers Say.

Manager.

"Having my people telecommute makes a big difference in the quality of work they produce. They get projects done on deadline and do a better job. I'm not just being a nice guy. One-minute commuting gives us more for our payroll dollar."

Supervisor/Manager.

"I'm in charge of a night shift with 20 word processors. Even though we paid extra, it was hard to recruit people and almost impossible to keep them after we had put in the resources to train them. Our absentee rates were always high. Although the neighborhood is safe in the daytime, no one wants to come here after dark. We just don't have the space for all our employees to be here during the day.

"When we heard about telecommuting, I jumped at the chance. All our people volunteered to set up a home office. We put in terminals and modem hook-ups. Our one-minute commuters can work anytime during the day so long as work is done on time and they agree to transmit it during the evening when the systems aren't loaded. They come in once every two weeks for lunch, a staff meeting, new assignments and updates on changes in procedures.

"We spent a total of three days in orientations, planning sessions and workshops with telecommuting consultants, and it really paid off. Most of the bugs were worked out before any of our people went home to work.

"During the past year since we began the program, no one has quit. Absenteeism is almost zero. The morale of my people is at an all-time high. They get more done with fewer mistakes and take pride in sending in a quality piece of work. I don't see how we managed to get along without telecommuting all those years."

Rules of the Road.

Success means following the ground rules. Here are the rules for successful telecommuting programs.

— *Telecommuters must be experienced.* Companies usually select employees they know — and who know the ropes.

— *One-minute commuters are employees.* They are salaried and have the same benefits as other employees.

— *Telecommuting work schedules are flexible.* Telecommuters spend some time during the week at the central office. Two to 3 days a week at home is common.

— *Telecommuting duration is flexible.* You might telecommute for just 3 months during a special project. You might work at home for several years because of children. You might stop entirely if your job changes.

— *Telecommuting is based on trust.* Your manager must trust that you will do your job. You must trust your manager to stay in touch and not forget about you.

— *Telecommuting requires training and planning.* You and your manager must plan, set goals, coordinate and measure your work both at the beginning and on a regular basis.

Driver Handbook for the One-Minute Commuter

In order to take

your work home,

you have to do your

homework.

*

Six Steps to Telecommuting.

— 1. *Check your job characteristics.* See what tasks can be done from home. Look for tasks that can be grouped and that don't need resources that can't be temporarily moved from the central office. (Job-Check)

— 2. *Check your own personality.* See if working from home is a good idea. Not everyone is cut out to work at home. (Self-Check)

— 3. *Make preparations at home.* Find work space and arrange work schedules with others in your household. Be sure your family is willing to accommodate your working at home. (Home-Check)

— 4. *Make preparations at the office.* Arrange for scheduling, work flow and communication with staff and clients. Be considerate. You don't want disgruntled co-workers. (Co-worker Check)

— 5. *Set up trial work-at-home days.* Look for a few strategic times when your willingness to work at home will help the company. (Telecommuting Trials)

— 6. *Set up a formal company pilot.* See if you can make telecommuting a regular part of the work schedule. (Telecommuting Pilot)

Brain surgery would not be a good telecommuting job.

Step 1 – Job-Check.
"Telecommutable" Tasks.

Characteristics of telecommuting tasks.

—*Require concentration:* reading, writing, planning, data entry, word processing, record-keeping, computation, data processing, analysis and review.

—*Need little face-to-face contact* and little supervision.

—*Have timelines and objectives:* Long projects that have defined milestones; Short projects with definite beginning and ending points.

—*Have simple requirements:* Need little support staff; Need simple or portable equipment; Need few or easily portable support materials.

—*Use technology:* Make use of telephone, computer or fax; Allow off-peak access to heavily used computer systems.

—*To do.* Break your job into a list of tasks. Analyze the tasks as if you were an outsider. Get rid of "assumptions" about how, where and when work is done now. List tasks you cannot do at home. List tasks you can do at home. Group them in telecommuting days.

1. Job-Check: Stay in Touch.

Information loops and social loops.

— *Meetings:* Training programs; Staff meetings for support, updates and esprit; Brainstorming and problem solving sessions; Impromptu meetings.

— *Contacts for information:* Casual conversations that share work experience; Contact with customers; Contact with supervisors and managers; Access to career advancement opportunities.

— *Contacts for relationship building:* Greeting people in the business community; Having lunches and coffee breaks; Participating in workplace social events.

— *To do.* Check the loops that are important to your job. Which can you obtain on the days you work in the central office? Which will you have to make special arrangements for? Is there a co-worker who will act as a buddy to keep you posted? How can your manager help keep you in the loop?

Step 2 — Self-Check.
Is Working at Home for You?

Knowing what you might miss is important.

— *Social interactions:* Socializing; Work interruptions; Daily face-to-face contact with customers; Daily face-to-face contact with managers; Going out to lunch daily; Planning social events; Coffee breaks.

— *Work support:* Co-workers that give daily work support; Daily access to files and equipment; Daily team work, synergism and brainstorming; Attending daily meetings.

— *Personal perks:* Dressing up every day; Being near shopping and businesses every day; Getting away from home every day; Enjoying office politics and gossip; Enjoying the daily commute to work.

— *Environmental perks:* Being in a pleasant, upscale workplace; Formal "at work" behavior; Formal office procedures; Signals for beginning and ending work.

— *To do.* Check those items you would greatly miss. *Do you need them every day?* This lets you know how many days a week to work at home. Start slowly with 1 day per week if you have a lot of checks.

2. Self-Check: Preferences.

Know what you might want to miss.

— *Social interactions:* Pettiness and gossip; Attending social events you don't enjoy; Political maneuvering and infighting.

— *Work interruptions:* Others who interrupt your work to chat; Co-workers interrupting to ask questions they could answer themselves; Too many unproductive meetings; Too many unnecessary meetings.

— *Environmental factors:* Unnecessary monitoring; High-pressure atmosphere; Having to look busy when the job is done; Noise, smoking or other distractions; Unpleasant surroundings such as impersonal decor.

— *Personal and financial factors:* Expense of going out to lunch daily; Dressing up every day; Being away from home every day; Commuting to work every day; Working at non-peak hours.

— *To do.* Check those items that greatly bother you. If there are several, you may want to work at home 3 or 4 days a week. If you have checked nearly everything on the list, you may be unhappy in your job and should consider finding a new one.

2. Self-Check: Work habits.

Telecommuter profile.

I like to work independently.
I write a to-do list for every workday.
I schedule my work ahead.
I try to solve a problem on my own first.
I call for help if I can't solve it quickly.

I trust myself to do a good job.
I find more to do when a job is done.
I know my job goals and objectives.
I keep in touch with my manager.
I take the initiative to contact others.

I know where and how to get supplies.
I know who has what information.
I know the written and unwritten
    rules.
I know who can make what decisions.
I know about promotions and benefits.

I enjoy working all by myself.
I enjoy teamwork and keep up my end.
I get my work done right and on time.
I know what jobs have priority.
I let my manager know when a deadline
    can't be met.

— *To do.* How many of these characteristics fit you? The more you counted, the better you'll do. (If you have trouble with overeating or overworking, be cautious about working at home.)

Step 3 — Home-Check.
Home Office Requirements.

What you need depends on your job.

—*Adequate work space:* A separate room or a partitioned part of a room (not the kitchen table); Good natural light, preferably with a window; Good ventilation; Away from household traffic and noises; Telephone jack and adequate electrical outlets; Soft general (overhead) lighting; Good locks on windows and doors.

—*Adequate furniture and fixtures:* High quality office chair; Sturdy tabletop surface or desk (not a folding table); Good incandescent lighting; Wall or desk lamps with fabric shades (task lighting); Locking filing cabinet.

—*Equipment* (your own or the company's): Telephone line and telephone; Computer or terminal; Surge-protector; Typewriter, printer, modem, fax or copier.

—*Supplies:* Duplicate software, printer paper, floppy disks; Stationery, envelopes, postage and office supplies; Reference books, telephone numbers; Duplicate files, appointment books.

—*To do.* Make a complete detailed list. Decide how you'll obtain these things.

3. Home-Check: Home Office.

Check insurance.

    — Homeowner's insurance usually doesn't cover home office equipment, but you can add an endorsement. If you are using company equipment, your employer may carry inland-marine insurance to cover equipment that travels with employees.

    — Auto insurance. If you're no longer driving to work daily you may be able to reduce your payments.

    — Workers Compensation Insurance. Your company's insurance should cover work related accidents wherever you work.

Check zoning and deed restrictions.

    — Your city or county office will have regulations about whether or not home occupations are allowed and under what circumstances.

    — Your deed or rental agreement could have covenants, conditions and restrictions that may restrict business use of the home.

    — *To do.* Check with your insurance agent and with your company's personnel department. (Restrictions on work at home are often ignored if no one is bothered.)

3. Home-Check: Family Needs.

Check with your family or co-dwellers.

— Discuss the new work arrangements with your family to get their cooperation.

— Visualize how things will change for better and for worse. Office space is no longer available for others to use. Work time at home is official work time (make rules about interruptions). Establish work hours and break times. Noise levels must be kept down. Establish realistic expectations about your accomplishing extras such as child care, errands, laundry and cleaning.

— Find out if someone resents the intrusion of business and work into the home. Will that person be home while you work?

— Evaluate personality clashes and family stability. Personal problems and family conflicts can make working at home impossible and make family conflicts worse.

— Ask family members for suggestions.

— *To do.* List all the pros and cons your family or co-dwellers found. List and discuss family suggestions. Can potential problems be managed? Is it *yes* or *no*?

Step 4 — Co-Worker Check.
Effects on others.

How everyday events might change.

— *Communications:* Answering telephone calls; Circulating memos and other internal information; Getting informal information; Reading bulletin boards; Posting hours.

— *Work flow:* Making work assignments; Sorting and delivering mail; Processing work before it goes to you; Processing work after you have completed your part; Reporting to you for assignments or supervision; Assigning work to you.

— *Decision making:* What to do about requests from customers and clients; How to handle special situations.

— *Record keeping:* Filing papers and having access to central or department files; Keeping time sheets, travel records, expense accounts, requisitions and payroll.

— *Work support:* Relying on you for help; Providing you with help; Making photocopies; Dictating and laser printing.

— *To do.* List the names of people whose work will be affected, who need access to you and to whom you need access. List ways to minimize effects.

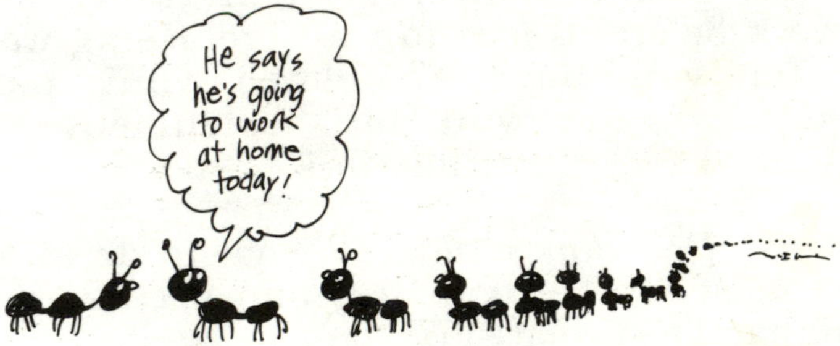
He says he's going to work at home today!

4. Co-Worker Check: Get Input.

Knowing co-worker response.

—*Ask how co-workers feel about:* You or anyone else working from home; Making changes in procedures; Things they like co-workers to do; Things they don't like co-workers to do; Tasks they particularly like; Tasks they particularly dislike.

—*Get advice from co-workers:* What changes would have to be made to accommodate your working at home? How many days per week can you telecommute without disrupting the work of others?

—*Ask what changes others will accept:* Acceptable ways to forward your telephone calls or take messages; Ways and times co-workers feel comfortable about calling you at home; Agreement about scheduling meetings so you can attend; Willingness to set due dates ahead of time; Remembering to keep you in the work flow; Agreeing to break longer projects into segments that you can take home; Helping out with pick-up and delivery of work; Understanding that it's OK for selected jobs to be taken home.

—*To do.* Check with co-workers to get their opinions, insights and support.

4. Co-Worker Check: Rewards.

Sweeten the pot.

— Offer to take home a job that a co-worker dislikes in exchange for one of your jobs that can only be done at the central workplace.

— Route telephone calls to a co-worker who enjoys answering them.

— Offer to take home rush jobs or unusual jobs that others might not like.

— Make your success at telecommuting a stepping stone for others to work at home in the future.

— *To do.* Think about what you can do for co-workers in exchange for their accommodating your telecommuting and add them to your list.

Then working from your original list of tasks, make a final list. Eliminate tasks which cause a great deal of change in the central workplace. Add tasks which would benefit your co-workers. Fine tune your list of special arrangements, materials, supplies and equipment needed for the tasks you have selected to do at home.

Step 5 – Telecommuting Trials.
Special Situations.

All companies run into situations that put them in a bind. When standard solutions to special situations are not satisfactory, there is often willingness to try new ways (such as telecommuting) to handle problems.

— Sick Leave. When your illness lasts a week or more, several days of your absence may be a recovery period when you are not well enough to travel to the office but are well enough to put in 3 or 4 hours of work at home. This recovery period is a good time to do some telecommuting.

Tell your manager which projects you are able to work on, what you expect to accomplish and during which hours you will be available by phone.

In this way the company saves the cost of hiring a temporary worker, saves the cost of paying sick leave for the hours you work and keeps work from getting too far behind. The company will also save downtime when you return because of the following: You have kept up on what is happening; Your recovery will be complete so you are no longer contagious to other workers; You return when you have the energy to do a full day's work.

5. Telecommuting Trials: Special.

—*Personal Leave.* Take home a folder of work you can do when you need to be away from the office for personal reasons. These include doctor's appointments, appliance repair or home deliveries that are only available during the work week.

—*Sick Child Care.* Some companies offer leave to take care of family needs while others do not. Very often working parents use their own sick leave, vacation or non-compensated time when their children are sick. Staying home to care for a sick child is comforting for both the child and the parent and offers an excellent opportunity for telecommuting.

When your child is sleeping or doesn't need constant care, you can get a great deal of work done. Take work home with you when you suspect that a child is becoming ill. If it's chicken pox, you can expect your child to be quarantined from child care or school for at least a week. Flu can last a week or more, and members of your family can come down with it over a period of several weeks.

Arrange for telephone contact and projects to work on. If there is a speaker phone in the office, you can even take part in staff meetings from home. Arrange to meet deadlines, identify specific tasks for completion and keep track of hours.

5. Telecommuting Trials: Special.

— *Parental Leave.* Begin telecommuting before the baby is born. This makes it easier to resume working at home part-time after the baby arrives. Your employer won't be without you entirely for several months and you will have some income during your leave.

— *Trip Reduction Ordinances.* To reduce traffic and clean up the air, cities, counties, regions and states are passing transportation ordinances. These laws require employers to reduce the number of single occupant automobile trips their employees make. Home telecommuting is an effective way to comply with these ordinances.

— *Special projects.* Many companies have peak times when there is more to do than can be done during regular work hours. Volunteer to work on a special project, a rush job or other overflow work at home as a way to demonstrate to your manager how well telecommuting can work.

If your company requires employees to put in a certain number of overtime hours, your manager will find employees more willing to work overtime if they can take the job home.

— *To do.* Make a list of special situations.

Step 6 — Telecommuting Pilot.
Company Program.

Establish a formal telecommuting pilot.

With steps 1 through 5, you can function as an informal telecommuter (sometimes humorously referred to as a "guerilla telecommuter") without belonging to a formal program. In the long run this can be an insecure position. Should you get a new manager, be assigned to a new position or get complaints from others who don't have telecommuting status, you could lose your permission to telecommute.

— *Informal Telecommuting.* One "guerilla telecommuter" reports, "It took me a year to weasel and work the cracks. One day I finally told them that I would be working at home if they needed to reach me. It's ten years later and I'm still telecommuting. I'm a big exception. When I got a new manager, I had to fight to retain my status. My company is very conservative and traditional, so I always keep a low profile."

— *Formal Telecommuting.* A formal program gives you official telecommuting status and makes it possible for others in the company to telecommute as well. It will provide your company with measurable benefits of telecommuting. Volunteer to pioneer a formal telecommuting program.

6. Telecommuting Pilot: Co. OK.

Do a company check.

Assess your chances for success. Certain indicators signal a company is ready, willing and able to change.

Maternity leave.
Flextime schedules.
Child care programs.
Parental leave.
Job sharing arrangements.
Cafeteria benefit plans.
Rideshare programs.

Up-to-date telephone system.
Office automation.
Personal computers.
Take-home computers.
Voice mail.
Electronic mail.

Overflow work is contracted out.
Employees sometimes take work home.
Part-time employees are hired.
Deadlines, milestones, objectives used.
Performance standards are in place.
Supervisors judge by results.
Surveillance is minimal.

— *To do.* List indications that your company is willing to change. How much support your manager gives to these is a clue to how receptive he or she may be.

6. Telecommuting Pilot: Reasons.

Convincing management.

You must convince your management that telecommuting solves problems for the company so there is a reason for making changes. Remember these benefits from the last chapter? Can you think of others?

Improved productivity by 15-30%.
Reduced office space costs.
Improved morale.
Increase staff without adding overhead.
Off-peak use of computer equipment.

Improved recruiting.
Reduced absenteeism.
Access to new labor pools.
Reduced relocation costs.
Less office socializing.
Fewer work interruptions.

Reduced turnover.
Reduced cost of training replacements.
Fewer commuting trips by employees.
Reduced need for parking space.
Incentive for overtime and shiftwork.

— *To do.* Research how telecommuting can solve problems for your company. Talk the list over with your manager and others in the company. Select those most important to your manager and company.

6. Telecommuting Pilot: Stages.

— *Presenting your case.* It will take more than one discussion to convince your company to endorse telecommuting. Plan your strategy to include lots of discussions. One telecommuter humorously said, "I 'harassed' my manager several times before he agreed to let me telecommute."

— *Introducing the idea.* During your first five steps, bring to work news and magazine articles about people who telecommute. Show them to your manager and co-workers. Post them on the bulletin board. Share your copy of this book. Bring up telecommuting at staff meetings. Start a task force.

— *Setting the Stage.* Suggesting a telecommuting experiment will make management more comfortable. A trial will alleviate fears of being stampeded by a horde of workers all wanting to telecommute. Begin with just 1 day a week and work up to 2 or more as telecommuting becomes comfortable for everyone. Make it easy to say *yes*.

— *Perservering.* Don't give up if at first you don't succeed. After all, buyers have to see or hear of a product seven times before they buy. Keep talking about the benefits of telecommuting. Make it hard to say *no*.

6. Telecommuting Pilot: Propose.

— *Write a proposal.* Give your manager a simple one-page proposal. This document and your trial telecommuting are valuable for discussing a pilot. Include:

> Benefits to the company.
> Telecommuting tasks and schedule.
> Why you are a good candidate.
> Why you want to telecommute.
> Why it will work in your company.

— *Create a written pilot plan.* Ask your manager for an OK to write out a short plan for the pilot for his/her approval. Include:

1. Purposes of the telecommuting pilot:
   Evaluate benefits/costs to company.
   Evaluate where/how it works best.
   Establish future guidelines.
2. Your telecommuting tasks.
3. How to measure your performance.
4. Your telecommuting schedule.
5. Methods of keeping in touch.
6. Beginning and ending dates of pilot.
7. Criteria for measuring success.
8. Date to assess expanding program.

— *Do-it-yourself pilot.* Consult the Driver Training section for excellent resources. Set aside time to plan the pilot carefully and to orient and train your people. Faithfully follow complete management guidelines.

Driver's Test for the One-Minute Commuter

"Getting tied up in traffic

Can put the brakes on business.

Consider an alternate route."

*

The Governor's
Conference on Telecommuting
Seattle, Washington, 1989

Telecommuters, Start your Engines

This chapter is for planning and testing your approach. It's an open-book test! By all means use your Driver Handbook.

Name_____

Address_____

_____

Phone— Home(___)_____

Phone— Work(___)_____

Employer_____

Employer Address_____

_____

Name of Supervisor_____

Position of Supervisor_____

Name of Decision-maker, if different

_____

Your Title_____

Your Job Function_____

_____

_____

Equipment you regularly use in your work.

_____

_____

_____

_____

_____

_____

_____

_____

Other resources you use in your work.

_____
_____
_____
_____
_____
_____
_____

Who will be affected by your working at home? How?

_____
_____
_____
_____
_____
_____
_____

Who would *support* your telecommuting? Why? How can they help?

_____
_____
_____
_____
_____

Who would *not* want you to telecommute? Why not?

_____
_____
_____
_____

Tasks you can do at home.

_____
_____
_____
_____
_____
_____
_____
_____
_____
_____

Tasks you cannot do at home. Why not?

_____
_____
_____
_____
_____
_____
_____
_____

Where in your home would your office be?

_____
_____

What furniture, equipment and supplies do you need?

_____
_____
_____
_____
_____
_____
_____

How does your family feel about all this?

_____
_____
_____
_____

How often and which days would be at home?

_____
_____

How will you track hours or work done?

_____
_____

How will your manager know you're working?

_____
_____
_____
_____

How will co-workers know you're working? Expect some teasing. Can you handle it?

_____
_____
_____

How will you stay in the loop?

_____
_____
_____
_____
_____
_____
_____

How do employees get promoted at work?

_____

_____

_____

List situations for your trial telecommuting.

Your personal time-off needs.

_____

_____

_____

_____

_____

_____

_____

The company's special work needs.

_____

_____

_____

_____

_____

_____

_____

Assess your chances for success:

Has anyone else in your company worked at
home? Who?_____
If so, for how long?_____
If so, how often? _____
If so, for what reasons? _____

_____

_____

_____

_____

What else indicates that your company might accept telecommuting (flextime, child care help, automation, goals, objectives)?

_____

_____

_____

_____

Is there a major change occurring in your company making it wiser to wait?_____
What change?_____
How long is the wait? _____

How long have you been with:

The company?_____
Your manager?_____
Your manager's manager?_____

How long has your manager been with the company?_____
How long has your manager's manager been with the company?_____

How well do you know the ropes?_____
Does your manager rate you as tops?_____

Do you think your manager will agree to your telecommuting?_____
Why or why not?_____

_____

_____

_____

_____

Check areas that your employer would like to improve. (How important is the area to your manager and to the company?)

M (major problem) S (smaller problem)
___ Lack of productivity
___ Employee turnover
___ Employee absenteeism
___ Employee tardiness
___ Crowded mainframe access
___ Hard to recruit the right people
___ Too much office socializing
___ Low employee morale
___ Many interruptions during work
___ Not enough work space or office space
___ High cost of work space or office space
___ Many employees with long commutes
___ Employee parking space problems
___ Unproductive staff meetings
___ Hard to fill shiftwork positions
___ Poor communication among staff
___ Lack of work performance standards
___ Other (Be specific)

_____

Your time plan for telecommuting.

Date for step 1 Self-Check_____
Date for step 2 Job-Check_____
Date for step 3 Home-Check_____
Date for step 4 Co-Worker Check_____
Date for step 5 Telecommuting Trials_____
Date for step 6 Telecommuting Pilot_____

Did you get your license to telecommute?__

Driver

Training

for Company

Programs

"Knowledgeable and competent

consulting services

is a key to success.

During the first year, the program

paid for itself in productivity alone."

*

DAVID FLEMING
Program Director
California State Telecommuting
Pilot

Choosing a Consultant.

When to call a consultant.

When your company is establishing a formal program, it is time to call in a professional telecommuting consulting firm. This is especially important if your company doesn't have the time and expertise for planning, training and following through on evaluating, expanding and training new telecommuters and their managers.

Telecommuting consulting firms specialize in establishing telecommuting programs for employers by offering executive briefings, needs assessment, program planning, staff orientations, training workshops for telecommuters and managers, ongoing evaluation, program adoption and expansion.

Those who have used the services of qualified consultants report that the expert guidance helped them design programs for success. Employers saved time, avoided pitfalls, set realistic expectations, generated necessary support, enhanced policy, provided essential training and established a foundation for assimilation of the program into the corporate culture. Costs of program implementation are generally recaptured in the first six months to one year. Thereafter, the telecommuting program saves money.

What to look for in a consultant.

A qualified telecommuting consultant is a management consultant who works well with people and has expertise in the following:

— Actual experience with telecommuting and several years of managing business from home.

— In-depth knowledge of all aspects of telecommuting: business and societal applications, history, and what to avoid.

— Experience in teaching adults and in developing and leading seminars and training workshops.

— Experience in working with management to plan, implement, evaluate and maintain telecommuting.

— Knowledge of and experience with management practices that are both result-oriented and people-oriented.

— Knowledge of available technologies that would be useful for the planned telecommuting project.

— Enthusiasm for and belief in telecommuting as a viable way to manage work.

Resource Guide.

The Electronic Sweatshop
1988, Barbara Garson
Simon and Schuster, NY
$17.95 through bookstores

Exploring the World of the Personal Computer
Jack M. Nilles
1982, Prentice-Hall, Inc.
Englewood Cliffs, New Jersey 07632

Micros and Modems:
Telecommunicating with Personal Computers
Jack M. Nilles
1983, Reston Publishing Company, Inc.
A Prentice-Hall Company
Reston, Virginia

Put Work in Its Place:
How to Redesign Your Job to Fit Your Life
Bruce O'Hara
Work Well Publications
620 View Street, Suite 521
Victoria, B.C.
Canada V8W 1J6.
$12.95 US postpaid

The One-Minute Commuter
How to Keep your Job and Stay at Home
Telecommuting
Lis Fleming, 1989, Fleming, LTD
Orders: Acacia Books
1309 Redwood Lane
Davis, CA 95616
(916) 753-1519
$9.95 + $2.50 shipping/handling
California add $.60 sales tax

Resource Guide.

The Telecommunications-Transportation Tradeoff
Options for Tomorrow
Jack M. Nilles
1976, John Wiley & Sons, Inc.
New York, London, Sydney, Toronto

*Telecommuting: How to Make it Work for You and Your
Company* (a complete management guide)
Gil E. Gordon and Marcia M. Kelly
Prentice-Hall, Inc.
Orders: Gil Gordon Associates
10 Donner Court
Monmouth, NJ 08852
$15.95 postpaid

Telecommuting Review, The Gordon Report
Gil E. Gordon
TeleSpan Publishing Corporation
50 West Palm Street
Altadena, CA 91001
(818) 797-5482,
Newsletter: telecommuting & workplace changes
$157 annually

Telecommuting: The Future Technology of Work
Thomas B. Cross and Margorie Raizman
Dow Jones-Irwin
Boulder, CO
through bookstores

Women and Home-based Work
The Unspoken Contract
1988, Kathleen Christensen
Henry Holt and Company, Inc., NY
$17.95 through bookstores

Resource Guide.

Working at Home: Is It for You?
William Atkinson
Dow-Jones-Irwin
Homewood, IL 60430
through bookstores

The Work-at-Home Sourcebook
Over 1,000 opportunities for work at home
Lynie Arden
Live Oak Publications
Orders: TWN Publications
242 E. Main Street, #38
Ashland, OR 97520
$15.95 postpaid

Working from Home: Everything You Need to Know about Living and Working under the Same Roof
Paul and Sarah Edwards
Jeremy P. Tarcher, Inc.
Los Angeles, CA
$12.95— through bookstores

The Worksteader News
Lynie Arden
TWN Publications
242 E. Main Street, #38
Ashland, OR 97520
Newsletter: opportunities for all kinds of work at home
$24 annually

"Computer sales will soar.

People will just take their work home

and get off the freeways

as traffic gets worse . . ."

*

GENE FARB
Whole Earth Access

Acknowledgements

Pioneers of telecommuting have forged onward with perseverance and patience. Wisdom found in these pages comes from them. I would like to acknowledge and give a public tribute to the following people:

Jack M. Nilles, father of telecommuting who first gave the concept a name in 1972, for painstakingly doing the masterminding and the tough research behind the scenes.

Laila P. Nilles, for her insistence on high standards and her support of telecommuting from the very beginning.

David M. Fleming, who first brought telecommuting home to roost, for making it happen for California state employees and many others around the country.

Gil Gordon, first telecommuting consultant, for keeping us all well informed over the years through his dauntless newsletter and sound advice.

Dick McIlvaine, guerilla telecommuter, for lending his artistic talent to these pages.

Martha and Harry Kohl, volunteer editors and proofreaders, for being terrific neighbors and foster grandparents.

Tova Fleming, who swears she'll never have a job with a desk, for keeping things in perspective.

Tom Miller, *Nick Sullivan*, *Lynie Arden* and *Joanne Pratt* for sharing their professional insights.

Grethe and Jens Svendsen for their support and encouragement.

The Telecommuters, pioneers all, for their enthusiasm, suggestions and stories.

The Managers, for taking the risks and assessing the rewards of leading their workers into the information age.

About the Author

Lis Fleming is a principal of Fleming, LTD and an active author, publisher, lecturer and telecommuting consultant. She has written numerous books and articles about telecommuting, computer-based home business, parenting and child care.

Positions held by Ms. Fleming include member of the advisory board for *Home Office Computing,* a national magazine; executive director of the Association of Electronic Cottagers on CompuServe; editor of *The Sacramento Venture*; advisor on telecommuting to numerous California government and civic organizations. She works with employers to establish telecommuting programs.

Ms. Fleming brings more than 15 years experience in homebased business to her work. A credentialed teacher, she develops and leads seminars for entrepreneurs of home businesses and training workshops for telecommuters and telemanagers.

The One-Minute Commuter, like her other works, helps people to improve the quality of their lives. Her books put hard-to-get facts based on real-life experiences at your fingertips. She makes step-by-step details easy to follow.

Ms. Fleming's books are researched, written and published from her home office in Davis, California, where she lives and works with her family.

A survey of families

in Davis, California

shows that 84 percent of parents

stay home from work or school

to take care of their children

when they are sick.

*

With telecommuting

parents can be productive employees

at the same time.

Dear Reader,

Would you like to be interviewed about your telecommuting? Hardly a week goes by without a call from a reporter, writer, researcher or university student asking for a telecommuter to interview. If I gave out the names of the telecommuters we know, they would never get any work done. But if I had a long list, no one would need to be called more than once or twice.

What do researchers want to know? What kind of work you're doing, what position you hold, the name of your city, why you want to telecommute, how often you work at home, what equipment you use in your home office, how long you've been doing this, what works and doesn't work.

It shouldn't take a lot of time. You might be asked for a photo. (One telecommuter not only had her picture in the local paper and a national magazine, but also appeared on the national television program *20/20*.)

If you're interested, send your name, phone number, mailing address and story about telecommuting to Fleming, LTD, P.O. Box 1738-TC, Davis, CA 95617-1738.

I'd love to have your story even if you don't want to be interviewed. Just write "Don't give out my name, but let me tell you all about my telecommuting."

I look forward to reading your story.

Best wishes, Lis Fleming